Celebrate
Jewish Festivals

Series editor: Jan Thompson

Angela Wood

Heinemann

First published in Great Britain by
Heinemann Publishers (Oxford) Ltd
Halley Court, Jordan Hill, Oxford OX2 8EJ

MADRID ATHENS PARIS FLORENCE PRAGUE
WARSAW PORTSMOUTH NH CHICAGO
SAO PAULO SINGAPORE TOKYO MELBOURNE
AUCKLAND IBADAN GABORONE
JOHANNESBURG

Designed by Sue Clarke
Illustrated by Jeff Edwards
Colour reproduction by Track QSP

Printed in Hong Kong / China

00
10 9 8 7 6 5 4

ISBN 0 431 06949 2

British Library Cataloguing in Publication Data
Wood, Angela
  Jewish Festivals. – (Celebrate Series)
  I. Title II. Series
  296.4

Acknowledgements
The author would like to thank these people for having
their picture taken, giving their views on the writing, or by
helping in other ways:

Joanna Bower Ish-Horowicz and her family; Amit Silverman
and his family; Jenny Buitelaar; Sheila Chiat; Samuel Gilmore;
Ester Gluck; Marcus Graichen; David Gryn; Rabbi Hugo
Gryn; Jean Hoffman and Wendy Williams, with their pupils;
Angela and Sasha Howard; Andrea Lawrance; Charles
Maxton of the Jewish National Fund; Rachel Ouseley; Philip
Ratner; Maxwell Simon; the children and teachers of Sinai
School; Kas Smith; Rabbi Mark Solomon; Carmella and
Raquel Stanbury; Steve Winston; and Rita, Jonathan and
Naomi Yusupov.

The Publishers would like to thank the following for
permission to reproduce photographs.

Guy Hall: p.4; Angela Wood: p.4; Guy Hall: p.6, p.7, p.8, p.9,
p.10, p.11, p.12, p.14; Circa Photo Library: p.15; Guy Hall: p.16;
Angela Wood: p.18, p.19; Trip: p.20; Guy Hall: p.21, p.22, p.23;
Circa Photo Library: p.24; Trip: p.25; Angela Wood: p.26; Guy
Hall: p.27, p.28, p.29, p.31, p.32, p.33, p.34, p.35; Angela Wood:
p.36, p.37, p.38, p.39; Guy Hall: p.41; Angela Wood: p. 42, p.43.

Cover photograph reproduced with permission of Zefa.

Details of written sources

Song for Friday, Forms of Prayer for Jewish Worship: Daily
and Sabbath, *Reform Synagogues of Great Britain*, Oxford
University Press, 1977: p.7; Tu B'Shevat Song, Forms of
Prayer for Jewish Worship: Daily and Sabbath, *Reform
Synagogues of Great Britain*, Oxford University Press, 1977:
p.27.

Our thanks to Denise Cush of Bath College of Higher
Education for her comments in the preparation of this
book.

Every effort has been made to contact copyright holders of
any material reproduced in this book. Any omissions will be
rectified in subsequent printings if notice is given to the
Publisher.

**For Amit and Joanna, who are my friends
and who made this book.**

Contents

The sun and the moon

This unit tells you about the Jewish calendar.

Amit on his father's shoulders.

Joanna in her home, eating hallah – special festive bread – on Shabbat with a close friend.

In this book, two children talk about the ways that they celebrate Jewish festivals and what they mean to them. They live in different countries and have never met. But they are both Jewish and that joins them together.

Joanna

Joanna is 9 and lives in south London with her parents, younger sister and two older sisters, who are twins. They are all at school. Joanna's father is a doctor and her mother runs a Jewish nursery school. They are all very musical and Joanna plays the recorder, piano and cello.

Amit

Amit is 12. He was born and lives in **Jerusalem**, the capital of **Israel**. His mother was born in Israel and grew up near the countryside. His father was born in America but came to Israel as a young man. Amit has two older brothers. Amit is good at drawing and painting, like his mother. He likes playing the drums with his music group, called 'Muza'.

> **The whole year is full of festivals and they all have a different feeling.**
> – *Amit*

Secular month	January	February	March	April	May	June	July	August	September	October	November	December
Hebrew month	Tevet Shevat	Adar	Nisan	Iyar	Sivan	Tammuz	Av	Elul	Tishri		Heshvan	Kislev-Tevet
Hebrew name (English name or meaning)	Tu B'Shevat (New Year for Trees)	Purim (Festival of Lots)	Pesach (Passover)	Yom Hashoah (Holocaust Day); Yom Haatzmaut (Israel Independence Day)	Shavuot (Pentecost or Feast of Weeks)		Tisha B'Av (Ninth of Av)		Rosh Hashanah (New Year); Yom Kippur (Day of Atonement); Sukkot (Festival of Booths or Tabernacles); Simchat Torah (Rejoicing in Torah)			Hanukkah (Festival of Dedication)

The Jewish calendar

The Jewish calendar is made up of 12 months. Each month begins when there is a new moon and lasts 29 or 30 days. The year is based on the sun and lasts about 365 days, so the 12 months do not make exactly a whole year. Most Jewish festivals are related to a particular season of the year. Because of the few extra days, the last month in the calendar is doubled every few years, so that the festivals fall in about the right season.

> **I shouldn't really say 'he' or 'she' or 'it' for God, because there isn't really a name for God.**
> – *Joanna*

When the festivals began

Some festivals date from about 3,200 years ago and are recorded in the **Torah**. They are the most important and are days of rest. Passages from the Torah are read about how the festival began, what happens during the festival and what it means. **Pesach** (spring), **Shavuot** (summer) and **Sukkot** (autumn) are all harvest festivals and are also about the story of the Jewish people being freed from slavery, receiving the Torah and living in the wilderness.

Two other festivals – **Purim** and **Hanukkah** – are about events in Jewish history that happened after the Torah was written. Other minor festivals have been added to the calendar as the Jewish community felt there was a need to mark some important events. Fast days are based on something sad that happened. Some festivals began only in the second half of the 20th century.

How festivals are celebrated

Family life is very important to Jews. All the festivals and fasts are kept at home, as well as at **synagogue**. Festivals give Jews ways to celebrate being together and to thank God for good things.

A festival a week!

This unit explains the meaning of Shabbat.

> **We work for 6 days and rest on the seventh. I find it a great relief not to have to go to school and work. Instead we go to the synagogue and then we come back home and I rest!**
> – *Joanna*

A mother and daughter lighting Shabbat candles.

Shabbat is the Jewish people's most special day. It is a day of rest, peace and joy. It starts on Friday evening just before it gets dark and it ends on Saturday night. Some Jews call it 'Shabbos'. Jews who keep Shabbat do not work on that day at all.

Freedom

Shabbat began about 3,200 years ago. The ancient Jews had been slaves in the land of Egypt and they knew how hard it was to work without rest. They came to believe that there are other important things in life as well as work. Everybody needs a time without work or worries, to be with their family and friends, just to be themselves, and to think about God. Jewish people have that time together.

Creation and holiness

Shabbat also helps Jews to think about the creation of the world. They believe that rest is something that God actually created. It is not just something that happens when people are not working. It is a special feeling of peace. That is why Jews call Shabbat holy. It means that it is a separate day, a day that is quite different from any other day.

Work and rest

Jewish teachers, called **rabbis**, said that there is more to rest than just not going to work. It would be good for Jews not to do work at home, either. They thought that if Jews had different ideas of what rest was, they might all celebrate Shabbat in different ways and then they could not really be together.

So they decided what work was: they said that working is making or breaking something. For example, writing is work but reading is not and picking a flower is work but smelling a flower is not. Today, technology helps Jews to keep Shabbat holy. They can use automatic timers to make lights or machines come on when they need them, so that they are not doing that work themselves.

The queen and the bride

Shabbat is about both actions and feelings. Sometimes Shabbat is called a queen, because she tells people what to do and Jews know what they should and should not do on Shabbat. Shabbat is also called a bride, because she is happy and full of beautiful feelings.

A song for Friday

This is part of a poem by a modern Hebrew poet, Bialik. It has been made into a song for Friday evening.

The sun on the rooftops is no
  longer seen.
Come out, let us greet the Sabbath,
  the queen.
See! She descends, the holy, the blessed,
Her messengers with her, of peace and
  of rest.

Welcome! Welcome the queen!
Welcome! Welcome the bride!
Peace be with you, messengers of peace.

" **For Jews who are used to Shabbat, it's not hard. Every time you go past a television and you don't turn it on, you keep Shabbat holy and you remember God.** "
– *Amit*

When he has said kiddush, this father pours wine from the main kiddush cup into smaller cups and glasses for everyone to share.

A taste of holiness

This unit tells you about celebrating Shabbat at home.

The father lays his hands on each child's head in turn and says: 'May God bless you and keep you.'

On **Shabbat**, Jews greet each other 'Shabbat shalom!' (Sabbath peace) or 'Good Shabbos!'.

Getting ready for Shabbat

In **Israel**, just before Shabbat, a loud siren is blasted in every town. By that time most Jews are already home, the shops have shut, buses have stopped running and the streets are almost empty. Outside, it is very quiet. In other countries where Jews live, most of the people are not Jewish. Outside, life goes on in the same way, but inside their homes, Jews are getting ready for Shabbat.

There is a lot to do and usually everybody joins in. Jews finish their week's shopping before Shabbat and try to buy nice things to have on that day, such as flowers for the table and their favourite food. They clean the house, polish the candlesticks and the wine cups and lay the table. They have a bath and put on clean clothes. Jews who keep Shabbat holy do not cook on that day.

Shabbat meals

There are three main meals on Shabbat: Friday evening; Saturday midday; and Saturday afternoon. There are three themes for Shabbat: God; **Torah**; and Israel, so each time of the day has its own theme, its own meal and its own kind of activity.

Friday evening theme: Israel; activity: being together in a happy mood.

Saturday midday theme: Torah; activity: talking about ideas, especially the Torah reading for that Shabbat.

Saturday afternoon theme: God; activity: being quiet, having a nap, reading alone or going for a stroll.

The father is shaking salt over the broken hallah – which his children can't wait to get their hands on.

Candles and kiddush

On Friday evening, the mother of the family lights two candles to welcome Shabbat. Other women and girls may light candles, as well. Then there is **kiddush**, when Jews sing blessings for the Shabbat, with a cup of wine or grape juice. There is also a kiddush on Saturday at midday. Kiddush means making something holy.

Hallah

At each meal, there are two plaited loaves of special bread called **hallah**. The three strands symbolise the three themes. When Jews lived in the wilderness, about 3,200 years ago, they had to gather their food, called **manna**, every day. On Friday they gathered a double amount so that they would not have to work on Saturday. The two loaves are a symbol of the double amount of manna.

> ❝ **I like Shabbat. It has a special mood, especially if you're religious. We have friends who are very religious, and it's very nice. They light a lot of candles and it makes Shabbat feel warm.** ❞
> – *Amit*

Prayer, study and being together

This unit tells you about Shabbat at synagogue.

Carrying a Torah is an honour and a pleasure: Jews often hug the Torah as a sign of affection and respect.

> ❝ **One of the special things about Shabbat is going to synagogue.** ❞
> – *Amit*

Jews think it is better to pray together, if they can. In some **synagogues**, men and women sit separately and children can sit with either. In other synagogues, men and women sit together.

Synagogue services

There are three synagogue services on **Shabbat** – Friday evening, Saturday morning and Saturday afternoon. On Friday evening, there are prayers and songs to welcome the Shabbat and **kiddush** is sung, just as it is at home.

The Torah

On Saturday morning, there is a **Torah** reading from a scroll. Every synagogue has an **ark**, a special cupboard which contains one or more Torah scrolls. Each scroll is covered in a decorative case or cloth, with a silver plate and pointer hung around it, and silver bells on top. It is taken from the ark and paraded around the synagogue. As it passes, people often bow to it or touch it with the fringes of their prayer shawl and then kiss the fringes. Someone takes the bells, the pointer, the plate and the cover off the Torah and carries it to the reading desk. People who read from the Torah use a long pointer, called a **yad**, which means a hand. This helps them to follow the words, which are very close together, without smudging the scroll with their fingers. After the reading, the cover, the plate, the pointer and the bells are put back. Then the Torah is paraded round the synagogue in the other direction and put back in the ark.

Before or after the Torah is read, it is raised high and shown in four directions, so that everybody can see it clearly.

"   **At synagogue, we have special services for children. We do plays about stories from the Torah. I like getting a letter asking me to read part of the service. I practise reading the Hebrew. When my grandfather is here from Israel, he explains every single word to me.**
    – Joanna
"

Amit can speak, read and write **Hebrew** very well. Now he is learning to read the Torah scroll, which is harder than ordinary writing. His father is teaching him musical notes for chanting the Torah. When Amit is 13, he will chant a portion in his synagogue and give a talk about its meaning. He and his parents talk about the ideas in his portion.

Prayer for peace

The children at Joanna's synagogue made a prayer book with help from some adults. This is one of their prayers.

Dear God,
We live in such a busy, noisy world. We need times in our life when all we can hear is our own breathing or a bird singing in the trees. Thank you for people that we don't always need to say something to. Thank you for this moment to stop and be still, to think, to wait, to pray and just be who we are.

Looking back, looking forward

This unit is about preparing for the New Year.

> **"I don't always remember things I do that are bad. I remember doing something wrong when I was at nursery but it was such a long time ago that I can't really say sorry now. I don't even know the nursery teacher any more. "**
>
> *– Joanna*

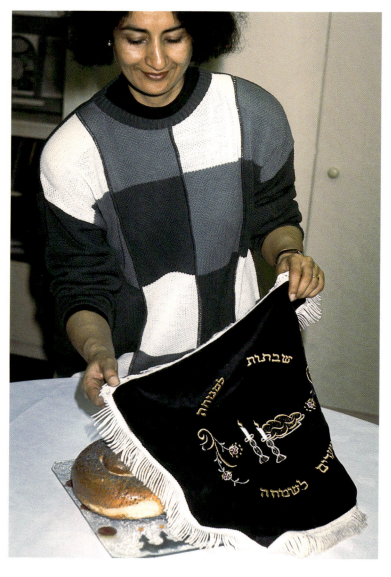

A mother prepares the table for the Rosh Hashanah (New Year) meal.

At some time, everybody does something that they are ashamed of. Perhaps they hurt someone else, or are lazy or waste things. Sometimes other people know about these things, but not always. Sometimes they are a secret. Jews believe that they should take time every day to think about what they have done or not done. If they have done something bad, or not done something good when they had the chance, they should try to be better. They also believe that if they are really sorry, God will forgive them.

This painting by Kas Smith shows a shofar – a musical instrument that is blown during New Year. The shofar is broken because it represents a broken heart.

Being sorry and saying sorry

Just before and during the time of their New Year, Jews think especially hard about what kind of person they are. They look back on the year that is just ending and try to be better in the year that is about to begin. They make an extra effort to put right something they have done wrong or to make up with someone they have hurt.

Jews believe that there are three things that they can do to help them start the New Year afresh:

t'shuvah being sorry and saying sorry to the person they have hurt, and saying sorry to God

t'filah praying

tzedaka doing good things.

" You have to be the best you can and it's hard. If you have a lot of sins, you feel bad. But our parents and teachers help us to make t'shuvah. "
– *Amit*

A story about t'shuvah, t'filah and tzedaka

A well-known and loved rabbi was passing a synagogue at this time of the year and the people asked him to come in. 'I can't!' he said, 'It's too full!'. The people replied that they would make room for him. 'I mean that it's too full of prayers!' he answered. 'The people inside don't really mean what they're praying. They're not praying about their lives. They're not sorry about anything they have done. They're not trying to be better and their prayers won't make a difference to how they behave. Their prayers should come out into the world, but they stay in the synagogue. That's why it's too full and I can't go in!'

The birthday of the world

This unit tells you about Rosh Hashanah – the New Year.

Rosh Hashanah means 'the head of the year', and is the **Hebrew** name for Jewish New Year. Jews greet each other with 'L'shanah tovah!' which means 'For a good year!'.

The **synagogue** services are quite like **Shabbat** services. There are extra prayers and songs for the day that help people think about their lives.

The shofar

There is also a part of the service when a horn, called a **shofar**, is blown many times. The shofar is probably the oldest instrument in the world that is still played today. It symbolizes many things. It is completely natural, just made of a horn from an animal (usually a ram), that is cleaned and hollowed out with a mouthpiece cut into the narrow end.

> ❝ **Rosh Hashanah celebrates the beginning of the year. We want the next year to be a blessed year and have a special big dinner. We eat apples dipped in honey in the hope that the next year will be a sweet one. We also bless all kinds of fruits.**
> *– Amit* ❞

Eating apples dipped in honey is a sticky business – but lots of fun!

Blowing the shofar in synagogue.

The shofar reminds Jews that they should be completely natural and honest with God. When the shofar is blown, it is held to the left side of the body, to show that its sound comes from the heart. The shofar is curved because people's lives are not 'straight' and they sometimes go wrong. When a shofar is blown, there are three basic notes, played in various combinations, that express the meaning of this season. Joanna's father is one of the people who blows the shofar in their synagogue.

The shofar notes

tekiah *a long blast with a clear tone – calling people to attention*

shevarim *a 'broken' sound, with three short calls – wailing or crying because hearts are broken*

teruah *an 'alarm', a series of fast, short notes – expressing the feeling of worry or fear*

> **The shofar is a bit like an alarm clock and it wakes us up to think about things. In the time of the Torah, they used to blow the shofar to make an announcement, especially if the king was coming. We say that God is like our king and feels very near to us. We can be especially close to God at this time. I think that God is inside me.**
> – *Joanna*

15

A time to be sorry

This unit is about Yom Kippur – the Day of Atonement.

Yom Kippur means the 'Day of Atonement'. **Rosh Hashanah** falls on a new moon, the first day of the month, and Yom Kippur falls on the tenth. The days in between are a time for Jews to think about their lives. Many Jews do not have parties or entertainment then. Jews believe that they should do everything they can to put right whatever they have done wrong. They should not just say sorry to God if there is something they themselves could do to make things better.

Fasting and not fasting

Yom Kippur is a **fasting** day that lasts from sunset to sunset. Saving life and being healthy are very important to Jews. No-one should risk their health by not eating and drinking. Jews who are sick or weak, pregnant women and mothers who are breast-feeding should eat and drink normally.

> " Adults don't eat or drink the whole day and it's hard. The trick is to get used to fasting bit by bit when you're small. Last year, I didn't eat until 3pm, and then I had pizza and a Coke. If you make it through fasting, you feel good. "
> – *Amit*

Undressing the Torah by taking off the bells, the pointer, the plate and the cover. For the season of Rosh Hashanah and Yom Kippur, the Torah coverings are white. Here, the cover is being changed.

" I don't have breakfast and I fast as much as I can. I wasn't allowed to fast when I was younger. I feel very grown-up when I fast. It helps me think of people who are starving. But I don't really know what they feel, because they haven't eaten for days and I haven't eaten for just a few hours, so it isn't the same. We fast so that we don't spend the whole time thinking about food. We think about God, instead. If we're sorry, God forgives us. "

– Joanna

Wearing white

Throughout this time, the **Torah** coverings and **ark** curtains are white, which is a symbol of purity. Many Jews also wear white clothes on Yom Kippur. Jews hope that the day will help them feel close to God and that they will be better in the coming year.

Synagogue services

Yom Kippur is serious but not sad. Some prayers are sung to very lively tunes because Jews feel that it is good to be able to say sorry to God, who is really forgiving. The **synagogue** services are the longest in the Jewish year. They begin in the evening, start again in the morning and go on all day. There is an extra service just before sunset. When Yom Kippur is over, there is one long **shofar** blast. It means that fasting can stop and Jews believe that forgiveness has come.

Saying sorry

This comes from the children's prayer book in Joanna's synagogue.

I didn't mean to be horrid and I'm not a nasty person. But I do feel awful about what I did and about not saying that I'm sorry. I want to say 'I'm sorry!' and it's so easy, really, yet the words won't come out. I know I'll feel better if I do. The longer I leave it, the worse it will get. So maybe I'll just take a deep breath, smile and say from the bottom of my heart, 'I'm sorry, really I am!'.

A wandering people and a shelter

This unit is about Sukkot – the festival of temporary homes.

Spending time in the sukkah.

> **Sukkot is a very rich and beautiful festival. Long ago, our people didn't have anywhere to sleep in the wilderness and so they made shelters from leaves and sticks. That's why we build a sukkah, too. I make pictures and things to decorate our sukkah and we eat there. My mother loves nature and she likes Sukkot very much.**
> *– Amit*

The festival of Sukkot comes on the fifth day after **Yom Kippur** and lasts just over a week. It is a treat after **fasting** and confession. Sukkot means 'huts' or 'tents'. After the ancient Jews left Egypt and before they entered the land of **Israel**, they wandered in the wilderness for 40 years. They made temporary homes, called sukkot (singular: **sukkah**). This was an important time in Jewish history. They faced many dangers but learned a lot about how to survive and how to trust God.

The sukkah

Most Jews today are lucky to have safe, comfortable homes. They need to feel close to that difficult time in their history so they actually live it again. Jewish families, if they can, build a sukkah in their garden or on the roof of their block of flats. They take their meals in the sukkah and some sleep there as well.

It can become their home during the festival. Most **synagogues** also have a big sukkah in the grounds or on the roof, where people eat and drink after services. Where Amit lives, most people live in flats and many families turn their balcony into a sukkah.

The sukkah roof

The most important part of a sukkah is the roof. It must be temporary and made of things that have grown but are not still growing. Branches and sprays of leaves are used for the roof. The roof must have a gap in it that is big enough for the sky to be seen. In Israel, it almost never rains during Sukkot, but in other countries it often does.

Sometimes the rain falls inside the sukkah!

The meaning of Sukkot

Sukkot is also the time of the autumn harvest festival and living in a sukkah helps Jews to feel close to nature. In many countries there are people without homes and Jews are especially aware at this time of the need to help the homeless.

Guests at Sukkot

Sukkot is a special time for hospitality and Jews like to have lots of guests in their sukkah. It is especially nice to have guests who are not Jewish, as Sukkot is a time for being open to other people. In the days of temples, people thought that there were 70 nations in the world. During Sukkot, the priest would make 70 sacrifices. Joanna's friend invites 70 guests to their sukkah – but not all at once!

“ In our friend's sukkah, when we have soup, sometimes the rain falls in it and our soup gets watery! We play in our garden and pretend it's the desert and our little sukkah is like the sukkot that our people built long ago. My younger sister and I act out the story and we say 'Look! The manna is falling!' Sometimes it's quite scary in the sukkah. It's very gentle when the wind blows and the dangling fruit sways. Once we made a gingerbread sukkah and decorated it with fruit shapes of marzipan. ”

– *Joanna*

Waving and shaking

This unit describes the four plants of Sukkot.

The four kinds of plants are an important part of the festival of **Sukkot**, and they symbolize many things. Often, all together, they are called the **lulav**:

lulav branch of a date palm – fruit which is good to eat but has very tiny flowers which have no smell and die quickly

hadassim spray of myrtle leaves – tiny fruit which cannot be eaten, but very beautiful flowers

aravot spray of willow leaves – no flowers and no fruit

etrog a citrus fruit, a bit like a lemon, with a straight side and a curved side, and a knob on top – both flowers and fruit.

" We buy the four kinds of plants at the market in Jerusalem. The best prices are in the afternoon just before Sukkot. We take the four together and wave them to the north, south, east and west, and up and down. One has fruit but no flowers, one has flowers but no fruit that you can eat, one has both fruit and flowers, and one has no fruit and no flowers. We feel sorry for it! "
– *Amit*

Jews take great care in choosing the plants of Sukkot.

The human body

The four kinds of plants can be compared to parts of the human body. The lulav (palm) is like the back: it means that Jews should always walk straight in the world and be able to hold up their heads in life. The hadassim (myrtle) leaves are shaped like an eye: they remind Jews to see clearly and with understanding. The aravot (willow) leaves are in the shape of lips: they tell Jews that they should speak truthfully and fairly. The etrog (fruit) is a bit like the heart: it asks Jews to have an open heart, full of kind and loving feelings.

> **" Daddy puts his hands over our hands when we wave the lulav and he pulls our hands to guide them the way we should wave the lulav. It sounds like rain. The etrog has a sweet smell. "**
> *– Joanna*

Different kinds of people

The four kinds of plants can also be compared to different kinds of people. Flowers are said to be 'beautiful' because they are lovely to look at and smell. People are 'beautiful' if they know a lot and have good ideas. Fruits are said to be 'useful' because they can feed people and are good for their health. People are 'useful' if they do good things and help others in their daily life. Like the four plants, some people are 'useful' but not 'beautiful'; some are 'beautiful' but not 'useful'; some are both 'beautiful' and 'useful'; some are neither 'useful' nor 'beautiful'. The community is made up of different kinds of people. They all need each other and should stick together. That is why the four kinds of plants are held together when they are shaken.

'We take the four together and wave them to the north, south, east and west and up and down.'

Going round and round

This unit tells you about Simchat Torah – rejoicing in Torah.

> **I like Simchat Torah. We march around the synagogue in the parade of the Torah scrolls. We have a mini Torah that's made of paper and all the children get turns in carrying that one. Then, in our synagogue, we have to close our eyes and some of the grown-ups have big bags of wrapped sweets. They throw the sweets everywhere. Then we open our eyes and we can scramble for the sweets!**
>
> *– Joanna*

Dancing with the Torah scrolls is a real joy!

Sukkot lasts for a week. It is a time for enjoying the fruits of the harvest and inviting guests into the **sukkah**. There is also a 1-day festival at the end, on the eighth day. This festival is part of Sukkot because Jews still use the sukkah but also not part of Sukkot because they do not shake the **lulav**.

The Torah circle

The eighth day comes just before the week when Jews will start to read the **Torah** again from the very beginning and will go on reading it bit by bit over the year. So the day marks the time when reading the Torah is finished and begun again immediately. A passage is read from the very end of the Torah and then a passage from the very beginning. This shows that the Torah never stops.

All the Torah scrolls in the **synagogue** are taken out of the **ark** and paraded around the synagogue, usually seven times – sometimes out of the synagogue and into the world, as well. People dance and sing and everybody is full of life. **Simchat Torah** means 'rejoicing in the Torah'.

❝ Simchat Torah is a very strong feeling. In synagogue, there are kids on people's shoulders and people are singing with great pride. We also go out into the street with the Torah scrolls, like a parade, and kids blow horns and wave flags.
– Amit ❞

One man's memory

Samuel Gilmore is 90 years old. His family was from Poland but, about 100 years ago, came to England, where it was safer. Now he lives in the USA. He says:

'I can remember my grandfather studying from a large book, even though he was partly blind. Every Shabbos (Shabbat), in my best clothes, I used to go with him to shul (synagogue). People respected him because he was so learned. He had the seat next to the ark, facing Jerusalem – a place of honour – and little Sammy sat beside him! On Simchat Torah, we read the end of the Torah and then started to read from the beginning all over again. He was the one who read the first part of the Torah. The ladies used to throw raisins and almonds as treats – and he would tell me to pick them up!'

Leaping for sweets at Simchat Torah reminds Jewish children that the Torah is full of sweetness.

Eight nights of light

This unit tells you about Hanukkah.

Hanukkah lasts 8 nights in the winter. It started about 2,200 years ago, when **Israel** was invaded by the strong army of the ancient Syrian Greeks. Unlike Jews, they believed in many gods and made statues of them. They worshipped their idols in the Jewish **temple** and spoiled many things there.

Lighting 8 candles on the hanukiah, with the shammash, on the last night of Hanukkah.

The Maccabees and the temple

There was a danger that some Jews might follow the Syrian Greeks and that the Jewish religion and way of life would die out. Many Jews could not stand up to the Syrian Greeks but a small group of Jews, the Maccabees, had the courage to fight back. Their numbers grew and they won. They cleared up the temple and set it right again. They needed some olive oil for the special seven-branched candle-holder. It seemed that they only had enough for one day, but it lasted for eight days, until more could be made. Hanukkah means 'dedication'. The temple was rededicated and the Jews dedicated themselves to God again.

The hanukiah

Each evening during Hanukkah, Jews light oil or candles on a special holder called a **hanukiah**. It has spaces for eight lights in a straight line, and the shammash candle to light the others. On the first night, one is lit; on the second night, two, and so on up to eight. The hanukiah is put in the window so that everyone can see it. It is called 'advertising the miracle'. Jews show that the spirit of God is stronger than the power of any army or government.

> **Our uncle made a hanukiah from lots of screws. We like to put white-blue candles in it. We have chocolate coins called Hanukkah gelt. We play the dreidl with gelt or raisins. We can eat as many raisins as we want!**
> – *Joanna*

The spinning top

The special Hanukkah game is a spinning top, with a **Hebrew** letter on each of the four sides. In Israel, it is called a sevivon and the letters are initials for 'A great miracle happened *here*'. Outside Israel, it is called a dreidl and the letters are initials for 'A great miracle happened *there*'. Players have sweets, raisins or coins. They take turns in spinning the top. When it stops, the letter that shows tells the player what to do. It can be: put one in; take everything in the pot; take half of the pot; or nothing happens.

Playing the dreidl.

> **Once I made a hanukiah out of bottle caps and one from clay. Our parents give us presents so they get poor and we get rich! Special foods for Hanukkah are things fried in oil – very fattening! – like jam doughnuts or crisp potato cakes, called levivot or latkes. In Israel, they sell doughnuts on the street and give them out at basketball games, which is the most popular sport. They light a hanukiah outside the Israeli parliament and at the beginning of basketball games in the evening.**
> – *Amit*

Little trees and strong hands

This unit tells you what happens at
Tu B'Shevat – New Year for trees.

Jews who live outside Israel often plant trees when they visit — even if they are small and the spade is heavy!

> " We plant little trees in the garden. At our synagogue classes on Sunday mornings, we can buy stickers and stick them on a card. When the card is full, it's sent away with the money. Then a tree is planted in Israel and we get a certificate. "
>
> – *Joanna*

In the **Hebrew** Bible, there are many sayings about the beauty of nature and trees are a symbol of life and goodness. For example, 'The righteous shall flourish like the palm tree, grow tall like a cedar in Lebanon' (Psalm 92).

The Torah

The wooden rollers on a **Torah** scroll are called 'the tree of life'. The Torah itself is also called 'the tree of life'. Just before or just after the Torah is read, many congregations sing, 'It is a tree of life to those who grasp it and those who hold on to it are happy' (Proverbs 3).

Jews and the land of Israel

Jews love the land of **Israel**, wherever they live. They were exiled from their land about 1,900 years ago when the Romans occupied it. Since that time, they have lived in many other countries. When some Jews returned to Israel, about 100 years ago, they found few trees or flowers there. They began to till the soil, plant trees and sow seeds so that the land would flourish. They believed that the ancient saying was coming true: 'the desert will bloom'.

Planting trees

Even now that Israel is a modern state, the work of protecting nature and planting trees goes on. Many Jews who live outside Israel want to give something to the land and feel joined to the people of Israel. They help to plant trees by collecting money and often plant trees themselves when they visit Israel.

How Tu B'Shevat is celebrated

Tu B'Shevat is a modern-day festival which falls in January. In Israel, the winter is passing and it is time to plant young trees. In Britain, it is still cold and it might snow on Tu B'Shevat! One of the customs of Tu B'Shevat is to eat parts of 15 different fruits – from Israel if possible – because the festival falls on the 15th day of the month.

A Tu B'Shevat song

This is a song written by Israel Dushman.

The almond tree blossoms
and a golden sun does shine.
Birds from every rooftop
announce the festive time.
Tu B'Shevat is here –
the festival of trees!

Planting trees in the garden of a Jewish primary school.

" **Tu B'Shevat is like a holiday for the plants and trees and we sing all kinds of songs about them. At scouts and at school, we go to the woods to plant trees and hope that they grow. We also make up bags of dried fruit at school and take them to old people, like a gift from the trees. Or we can just give the fruit out to people on the street.** "

– Amit

Masks, make-up, making merry

This unit is about the festival of Purim.

Ester and Mordehai

Over 2,400 years ago, there were Jews in Persia. Ester was an orphan who was brought up by her uncle Mordehai. The king married her, but did not know that she was Jewish. Haman, his chief minister, was angry because Mordehai would not bow down to him. He knew that Mordehai was Jewish and he wanted to get back at all the Jews. He told the king that the Jews did not obey the laws, were not loyal to him and should all be killed. The king agreed, and signed and sealed the order. They drew lots to choose the day to kill the Jews. **Purim** means 'lots'. Haman built gallows to hang Mordehai and other Jews.

Reading the story of Ester on Purim morning at a Jewish primary school.

> **We have a fancy dress parade in synagogue. My grandmother in Israel makes us wonderful outfits. One year, all the children were characters from the story and Mummy and Daddy were wrapped up like the Scroll of Ester. When they unrolled themselves, we came out! We cook hamantashen cakes at home sometimes, too. We take gifts of food, called shalah manot, to elderly people.**
>
> *– Joanna*

> **Purim is a bit like Hallowe'en. We don't go trick-or-treating but we give each other shalah manot with all kinds of nice things, like sweets. All the kids and adults dress up any way they want, but it doesn't have to be scary. This year I did plaits and coloured braids in my hair! When I was 9, I dressed up as a joker. Purim is fun, a free day. You don't have to do this or that or not do this or that. The younger you are, the more fun Purim is!**
>
> *– Amit*

Definitely not school uniform, but fancy dress for the day!

How the people were saved

When Mordehai heard about this, he asked Ester to help. She had to tell the king that she was Jewish and asked him to change the order. She took a big risk. The king said that he could never change an order but he gave another order – that the Jews were free to defend themselves. They saved their lives and the king had Haman hanged on the gallows that he had built for Mordehai. When the Jews knew that they were safe again, there were parties everywhere. They gave each other presents and sent food to the poor.

How Purim is celebrated

The main part of the celebration is reading the story in **synagogue**, from the Scroll of Ester. This is quite like a **Torah** scroll but it has only one roller. Haman represents evil. When his name is read, everybody tries to drown it by booing and hissing, stamping their feet, waving a rattle called a gregger or ra'ashon, or in any other way they like. This is a way of showing that they want to get rid of evil in the world. One of the special foods for Purim is called oznei Haman ('Haman's ears') or hamantashen ('Haman's pockets'). These are triangular pastries, shaped a bit like an ear and stuffed, a bit like a pocket, with poppy seeds or fruit.

A time to be free

This unit tells you about Pesach –
the story of freedom.

In this picture by Philip Ratner, the soldiers are on the Egyptian side of the water and the Jews are crossing the sea.

> **It isn't nice for anyone not to be free. We celebrate getting out of Egypt where we were slaves a very long time ago.**
> – *Joanna*

Over 3,200 years ago, the Jewish people, called Hebrews or 'children of **Israel**', lived in Egypt. The ruler, called the pharaoh, made them his slaves. He said that if his country was at war they might join his enemies, so he had the Hebrew baby boys killed.

Moses

One **Hebrew** mother hid her baby, Moses, in a basket on the river. Pharaoh's daughter found Moses and took him to the palace. His sister had been watching all the time and told her that she knew a woman who could breast-feed him. It was Moses' mother! Perhaps she was able to tell Moses who he really was and where he came from.

Moses and God

When Moses grew up, he felt closer to the Hebrews than to the Egyptians. Once, he was so angry at a slave-driver who was beating a Hebrew that he killed him. He was scared of being caught and ran away, but he heard God telling him to return to his people.

Moses kept asking the pharaoh to let the Hebrews go but he refused. Terrible things happened to the Egyptians, but not to the Hebrews. These were the ten plagues. At first, the pharaoh did not see them as a warning, but in the end, he ordered the Hebrews to leave. They had to leave that night, in a hurry, so they baked their bread dough without letting it rise. It turned out as flat, unleavened bread.

The escape

A week later, the Hebrews reached the sea. The pharaoh had changed his mind and sent soldiers after them. The Hebrews crossed the water safely, but the Egyptians drowned.

The meaning of Pesach

This is the most important Jewish story, which many Jews see as the beginning of their history, when they became a free people. Jews are sad about the Egyptians who died, because they themselves were not to blame, and because there is good and bad in everyone. At the Passover supper, or **seder**, Jews call out the ten plagues. For each one, they spill some of their wine because they cannot be really happy about their freedom when other people died.

Shops in areas where Jews live stock foods for Pesach and display them in the windows.

> **They say that when the plagues came, the Jews put blood on the Hebrews' doors so that God could tell who was living there. But God could tell anyway!**
> – *Amit*

The ten plagues

The ten plagues that affected the Egyptians were:
blood; frogs; lice; wild beasts; sickness; boils; hail; locusts; darkness; and the death of the first-born child.

Everything is changing!

This unit is about preparing for Pesach.

> **You can't eat anything that's like bread. It's not really hard because you do eat but it gets to be a drag not to eat hametz all week.**
> – *Amit*

Pesach (Passover) falls in spring and lasts a week. The weeks and days leading up to it are the busiest time in the Jewish year. Jews need to feel that they are reliving the story of their ancestors in their own lives and that they themselves are also slaves who were freed by God.

Covering kitchen work-tops with foil, to make them free of hametz.

Hametz

The preparations are all about removing every single bit of **hametz** and not eating any of it during Pesach. Hametz means anything that is leavened or risen, such as bread, pasta, ordinary cakes and cereals, yeast extract and drinks with yeast such as beer. This is because of the unleavened bread that the ancestors took with them on the night of their escape.

Removing hametz

Jews also clean their homes thoroughly to remove any traces of hametz that might have fallen somewhere, such as biscuit crumbs in the bed! They also use dishes that have no hametz on them. Many keep crockery and cutlery especially for Pesach.

Otherwise, they can make some of it right for Pesach. Metal dishes can be boiled. Glass is non-porous; that is, it doesn't allow anything to pass into it, and can be soaked in clear water to be ready for Pesach. China and earthenware crockery is porous and cannot be made right for Pesach. Some Jewish families use disposable dishes during Pesach, as well.

Matzah

Jews eat unleavened bread, called **matzah**, during Pesach. It is very hard to make and today it is made in bakeries and factories, as it has to be just right. It is made only from flour and water, with perhaps some salt, and no yeast or raising agents at all. It must be made in 18 minutes from start to finish as, after that, the dough would start to rise. It turns out like a very crispy cracker with little air holes all over it. It comes in all sizes, either round, square or rectangular.

New clothes

Many Jews also like to have new clothes for Pesach or to save something new and wear it for the first time at Pesach. This is not because there might be hametz in their clothes, but because Pesach is a time of feeling fresh and new – like a slave who has just escaped.

The hametz treasure hunt, using a candle to see clearly and a lulav to scoop the hametz into a wooden spoon.

" **We're cleaning the whole time! We have to dust our own bedrooms. We wash and wipe everything. We have to get rid of the hametz. I miss pasta, but there are some nice cereals that we can have in Pesach. Everybody in the family works hard to get ready for Pesach. My older sisters help to make the cutlery kosher (right) for Pesach with boiling water. We have special dishes that we just use for Pesach. We put our ordinary ones in boxes and put them in the garage. We don't open the garage during Pesach so that we don't let the hametz in. Pesach is a bit funny.**
– Joanna "

So many questions!

This unit decribes the seder.

The **seder** is the supper on the first evening of **Pesach**. It is like a celebration banquet for free people. It is also like a play about the escape from slavery. Seder means 'order', and things happen in a certain pattern. Everybody reads, sings or follows from a book called the **haggadah**.

Usually, there are a lot of people at the seder and it is quite squashed, but nobody seems to mind.

When each of the ten plagues is recited, Jews flick off a drop of their wine or grape juice. They are sad about what happened to the Egyptians and so they spill a bit of their joy.

The parts of the seder

The seder has two parts, with a big meal in between. The first part is about the past. It begins with the youngest child or children asking questions about the story of Pesach. The second part is about the future, with hopes that everyone will soon be free. Many families go on singing and talking about freedom, often very late into the night.

Special foods

The table is laid with foods that are linked with Pesach. Many are on a special seder plate, that is used only on this night.

There is a glass or cup at everybody's place. People drink wine or grape juice four times. There is also a cup for the prophet Elijah. In the second part, this cup is filled and the door is opened in the hope that he will enter. There is a legend that he will one day announce that the **Messiah** has come and the world will be at peace.

There are three matzot (the plural of **matzah**) in a layered cloth. In the first part of the seder, the afikomen, half of the middle matzah, is hidden. When it is found at the beginning of the second part of the seder, it is shared out.

Karpas is a vegetable. Many families use a green vegetable, such as parsley, as a symbol of springtime and new life. Everybody eats a piece dipped in salty water to remind them of the slaves' tears and sweat.

Maror is a bitter vegetable, such as horseradish. Everybody eats a piece to remind them of the bitterness of slavery.

Haroset looks like the mortar which the slaves used in building. It is usually made of apples, honey and nuts, and tastes sweet. The maror is also eaten with haroset because there was a happy ending to their story.

The happy winner in the hunt for the piece of matzah.

" The grown-ups have a big discussion but we don't. Once Daddy marched around with some matzah in a bag on his back. My older sisters asked questions and he answered them. I read the part about the four kinds of children: wise, wicked, simple and the one who does not know how to ask. Mummy does funny actions with her hands and pulls faces to show what each of them is like. I like having a seder on the second night of Pesach, too, because two is double fun! This year we hid the afikomen and Daddy found it, but he still gave us a prize for hiding it in a good place! "
– Joanna

A time to remember

This unit describes Yom Hashoah.

The Avenue of Trees at Yad V'Shem. Some people have placed stones beneath the tree because it is a Jewish custom to leave a stone on a grave when visiting it, and the tree is like a memorial to the righteous person.

" **Yom Hashoah is a day to remember the shoah, the Holocaust, when six million Jews were killed by the Nazis. That's more than all the Jews today in Israel! There were about two million kids of my age or even less. They were all killed in a very cruel way, often in gas chambers. On Yom Hashoah in Israel, we have a special assembly at school. There's a siren all over the country and we stand silent and still, everybody at the same time.** "
– Amit

Remembering the shoah

Jews remember the **shoah** in many ways. Many of the people who died are unknown and they cannot be named. But wherever they are known, their names are recorded and recalled. Often, their names are read in between the words of a memorial prayer. They do that at Joanna's **synagogue** at their **Yom Hashoah** service.

Hope

In Hyde Park, in the centre of London, there is a huge slab of stone in memory of the shoah. Children and adults gather there to express their feelings of sadness and also to become strong enough to stand up to anything like the Nazi power again.

Rabbi Hugo Gryn often leads this service. He and his whole family were taken to a death camp when he was a teenager. He was with his father and luckily he himself survived. He says that what really helped him was his father's words about keeping up your spirits, 'You can live three weeks without food. You can live three days without water. But you cannot live three minutes without hope'.

People who helped Jews

In **Jerusalem**, there is a very large memorial centre called Yad V'Shem. One of the important places in it is an avenue of trees, each one planted in the name of someone who helped Jews during the shoah. One of those who risked her life to help Jews was Miep Gies, in Holland. She brought food and other things every day to Anne Frank and her family, who were in hiding. Anne kept a diary and left it behind when the Nazis took her and her family away to death camps. Miep saved Anne's diary and it was published after the shoah. When Miep was asked why she helped the Jews, she replied, 'It was far easier to help them than to live with the thought of them having no-one to turn to'.

66 **My grandfather comes from Poland. All his family died in the Holocaust except for one brother, who escaped. My grandfather was already living in the land of Israel. He had a happy life. He felt so bad when he heard about what happened to his family and he imagined how it was for them. Yom Hashoah is important for remembering the six million Jews who were killed. We think about them and then they're alive in our memories. If you don't think about them, they're dead in your memory.** 99
– *Joanna*

This sculpture at Yad V'Shem shows a man praying. People have placed stones in the folds of his clothes and around the base of the sculpture.

The people and their land

This unit describes the festival of Yom Haatzmaut.

Opposite the Western Wall in Jerusalem, flags are blowing in the breeze. The Israeli flag has blue stripes on a white background, like a prayer shawl, and also a blue star in the middle.

We have lots of flags of Israel and we put up pictures of Israel.
– *Joanna*

Hopes of Zion

In 1897, in Switzerland, there was an important meeting of Zionists. They talked about their hopes and plans for a Jewish state. Herzl, their leader, said, 'If you will it, it is no dream – to be a free people in our land, the land of Zion, Jerusalem'. This saying has been made into a song, which Jewish children often sing, especially on Yom Haatzmaut.

The Jewish people and the land of Israel

The Jewish people entered the land of **Israel** about 3,200 years ago. They believed that God had given it to them and they loved it very much. King David made **Jerusalem** their capital and they built a beautiful **temple** there. Jerusalem was built on Mount **Zion**. Zion stands for building God's kingdom in the world. Many Jews call themselves **Zionists**. They believe that Jews need Israel and have a right to live there.

Exile

About 1,900 years ago, the Romans defeated the Jews and they had to settle in other countries. They were never together in one place again. They longed to return to Israel, where they really belonged, and to start Jewish life there again.

Return

Over 100 years ago, groups of Jews from eastern Europe bought land in Israel. They lived together in small communities called **kibbutzim**, where they shared what they had and lived from what they grew. Arabs had been living in the land for centuries, under the rule of other countries. Many did not like the Jews returning and there were many battles.

After the **shoah**, the leaders and people of some countries were sorry about what had happened. They agreed with the Jews that they should have their own country. In 1948, the State of Israel was created. Jews in Israel and other parts of the world celebrated **Yom Haatzmaut**, Independence Day.

Peace in the land

Israel has had many wars since then. Many Israelis and Jews elsewhere want to make peace with the Arab people who live in or near Israel. Some of them think that it is worth giving up some of the land if it will bring peace.

The national anthem

The Jewish national anthem, HaTikvah, means 'hope'.

As long as in our hearts
there is a Jewish spirit
and our eyes turn to the east,
gazing at Zion,
our hope is not lost –
the hope of two thousand years,
to be a free people in our own land,
in the land of Zion,
in Jerusalem.

" **The day before Yom Haatzmaut, there is a memorial day for soldiers who died in the wars in Israel. Yom Haatzmaut is my favourite festival of all. We celebrate the birth of the new state of Israel. Some people hang Israeli flags outside their windows. In Jerusalem, everyone goes to the centre of the city. There are no cars and people are in the streets. There are parades, and fireworks in the square.** "
– *Amit*

A Jewish child in Israel created this picture of peace between Christians, Jews and Muslims.

Flowers on the mountain

This unit describes the holiday of Shavuot.

> **Shavuot is a holiday about how we got the Torah and everyone went to Jerusalem with fruit. In Jerusalem, some people hang fruit in their homes.**
>
> *– Amit*

The **Torah** was given to Moses, for the people, on Mount Sinai, when they were wandering in the wilderness. Jews believe that God revealed the Torah and goes on revealing things to people. The Torah became the Jews' special book, which they read each week, and which some Jews study every day.

The Ten Sayings

The **Ten Sayings** (sometimes called the Ten Commandments) are a very important part of the Torah. Most **synagogues** have them – or just the first words of each one – on the wall, near the **ark**.

Philip Ratner's picture of the giving of the Torah shows Moses, the two tablets on which the Ten Sayings were written, two shofarot and the first letter of the Hebrew alphabet in a fiery sky.

How Shavuot is kept

Shavuot was first a summer harvest festival. Many Jews bring fruits to their synagogue, just as they did in the days of the **temple**, to be given to people who need them. Synagogues are often filled with flowers, because it is said that, when the Torah was given, Mount Sinai was so happy that it burst into flower.

It is said that the people were awake all night, eagerly waiting for the Torah. Many Jews who love the Torah and want to understand it stay up all night to study on Shavuot.

A Shavuot party with plenty of cheesecake.

> **Shavuot is about when we got the Ten Commandments and people used to take a tenth of their crops to the temple for a sacrifice. The Torah has many important stories in it.**
> – Joanna

The particular foods for Shavuot are things like cheesecake and cheese-filled pancakes. There are many reasons for eating dairy food. One is that whipped cream looks like the peaks of Mount Sinai. Another is that the Torah is as nourishing for Jews as milk is for a baby.

The ten sayings

1. I am the Lord your God who brought you out of the land of Egypt, out of the camp of slavery.
2. You shall have no other gods but me…
3. You shall not use the name of your God falsely…
4. Remember the Sabbath day and keep it holy…
5. Respect your father and your mother…
6. You shall not murder.
7. You shall not commit adultery.
8. You shall not steal.
9. You shall not give false evidence against your neighbour.
10. You shall not envy … anything that is your neighbour's.

Breaking down and building up

This unit tells you about the fast day of Tisha B'Av.

> **They say that the Messiah may be born on Tisha B'Av and will come on a donkey. He is supposed to wake up the dead. Some Jews think that for the Messiah to come you need most of the Jews in Israel, but most are outside. I think he'll be born as a human and then some day reveal himself. Then we'll all have a great life! I believe in it, but it's hard to imagine!**
>
> *– Amit*

Two temples

Jews have had two **temples**. The first was destroyed by the Babylonians about 2,600 years ago. After 70 years, the Jews were able to rebuild it. The second one was destroyed about 1,900 years ago by the Romans, and has not been rebuilt. Jews practise their religion today in homes, **synagogues**, schools, youth clubs and other groups.

The Western Wall is the last remaining wall of the ancient temple in Jerusalem. It is a place of prayer for Jews from all over the world.

How Tisha B'Av is kept

Tisha B'Av is a fast day and comes in late July or August. It recalls the destruction of the temples, which happened on the same day of the year. Many other sad things happened to Jews on the same day.

The book of Lamentations is read or chanted to a very mournful tune and some Jews sit on the floor, as a sign of sadness. Lamentations speaks about the sorrow of the people who saw the first temple and much of the city being destroyed. Jews who hear it also remember some of the other sad events.

The days of the Messiah

Jews believe that the world as we know it will end one day and then there will be a time of peace, love, joy and justice which lasts forever. There are legends that God will send the **Messiah** to make this happen and that the Messiah will be a descendant of King David. The Messiah is described in many ways, such as a little child and a prince of peace.

Jews today have their own ideas about who or what the Messiah will be like. No one knows who or where the Messiah would be. Some say that every pregnant woman might be carrying the Messiah. Jews think more about the days of the Messiah and what life will be like then.

For many Jews, every good deed can help to bring the Messianic age nearer. This child collects money regularly for charity.

" The Messiah might come and make the world better. I believe but I've got my doubts. Sometimes I think I can't wait for the Messiah, but then I think it might not happen. We can help it come by being good. You would know that the Messiah had come if there were only good things and no bad things. I don't think the Messiah will be a person but a bit like a spirit. It won't be like a fairy with a magic wand and there won't be a big explosion in the air. It will happen slowly, not suddenly. Then my great-great-grandchildren, if I have any, would never have anything bad happening to them like someone saying 'I'm not your friend and I'm not going to play with you'. "

– Joanna

Glossary

ark the special cupboard in a synagogue which contains the Torah scrolls; it is usually on the western wall of the synagogue

fasting not eating or drinking, wearing leather, washing unnecessarily, putting on perfume or make-up or having sex

haggadah the book used at the seder

hallah (the 'h' at the beginning is pronounced in the throat and the word is sometimes spelt 'challah') special festive bread. On Shabbat the loaves are usually plaited (plural: hallot)

hametz (the 'h' at the beginning is pronounced in the throat) any foods which are leavened (risen), that is, made from fermented grain. Jews do not eat hametz during Pesach, and they clear their homes of it beforehand

Hanukkah (the 'h' at the beginning is pronounced in the throat and the word is sometimes spelt 'Chanukah') festival lasting 8 days in the winter

hanukiah (the 'h' at the beginning is pronounced in the throat) a holder for eight candles, plus the shammash, or 'servant' candle used to light the others. The candles are lit every night during Hanukkah. It is sometimes called a Hanukkah menorah

Hebrew the main language spoken today in Israel; the language of prayer and religious study for Jews everywhere

Israel the Jewish homeland and the modern Jewish state; often refers to the Jewish people

Jerusalem the capital of Israel; the site of the ancient temple; a place of pilgrimage for Jews

kibbutzim group settlements or agricultural communities in Israel

kiddush from the word meaning 'holy'; saying blessings for Shabbat or a festival, with wine or grape juice

lulav a date palm; one of the four plants of Sukkot

manna food which the ancient Hebrews gathered in the wilderness and which mysteriously appeared every morning

matzah unleavened bread, like crackers, eaten at the seder and, instead of bread, throughout Pesach

Messiah the person or spirit that Jews believe will bring a time of joy, peace, love and justice when the world ends

Pesach (the 'ch' at the end is pronounced like an 'h' in the throat) the spring festival of Passover that celebrates freedom

Purim meaning 'lots'; the festival in early spring that marks Jews being saved from destruction in ancient Persia

rabbi a Jewish teacher. Most rabbis lead part of the services and give advice to individuals; some congregations have male or female rabbis but most only have male rabbis. The teachings of the rabbis in ancient days are used by Jews today

Rosh Hashanah the Jewish New Year, which falls in autumn

seder the Pesach supper held on the first evening and by many families also on the second night

Shabbat sometimes called 'Shabbos'; the Jewish sabbath, a weekly day of rest which lasts from Friday evening to Saturday evening

Shavuot the early summer festival which celebrates the giving of the Torah

shoah the Holocaust, when six million Jews and many other people were killed by the Nazis

shofar (plural shofarot) a musical instrument made from the horn of an animal, usually a ram; blown in the New Year period

Simchat Torah (the 'ch' in the middle is pronounced like an 'h' in the throat) the autumn festival at the end of Sukkot, when the Torah is celebrated

sukkah (plural: sukkot) a hut or tent in which the ancient Jews lived while wandering in the wilderness

Sukkot the autumn festival when Jews build and live in temporary homes, to relive the experiences of their ancestors

synagogue a place of Jewish community worship, study and meeting

temple the ancient Jewish place of worship, where priests made sacrifices. The second temple was destroyed in the year 70 and has not been rebuilt; most Jews in north America call synagogues 'temples'

Ten Sayings sometimes called the 'Ten Commandments'; the basic rules for Jewish living

Tisha B'Av a fast day in late summer to recall the destruction of the temple and other sad events

Torah Jewish 'teaching'; the scroll containing the first five books of the Hebrew Bible; also appears in book form. A portion or passage of the Torah is read every week in synagogues and there are also portions for the main festivals

t'shuvah being sorry; asking for forgiveness and trying to be better

Tu B'Shevat the New Year for trees, which comes at the end of winter

tzedaka doing good things, such as being kind and thoughtful, giving money to charity or helping with a social project

yad meaning 'hand'; a pointer, usually silver, in the shape of a thin arm with a pointed finger, used to follow the words of the Torah scroll

Yom Haatzmaut Israel Independence Day, which comes in early summer

Yom Hashoah the day in spring when Jews remember the shoah and mourn those who died in it

Yom Kippur the Day of Atonement; a day of fasting and confession, which comes in the autumn

Zion the mountain on which Jerusalem is built, a symbol of God's kingdom in the world

Zionists people who believe that Jews need Israel and have a right to live there

Further reading

Non-fiction

World Religions: Judaism, Angela Wood; Wayland Ltd, 1995

Religion through Festivals: Judaism, Clive Lawton; Longman, 1989

Discovering Sacred Texts: The Torah, Douglas Charing; Heinemann Publishers (Oxford) Ltd., 1994

The Jewish Kid's Catalog, Chaya Burstein; The Jewish Publication Society of America, 1983

A Kid's Catalog of Israel, Chaya Burstein; The Jewish Publication Society, 1988

The Shabbat Catalogue, Ruth Brin; Ktav Publishing House, Inc., 1978

Jewish Holiday Crafts, Joyce Becker; Bonim Books, 1977

The Animated Megillah: a Purim Adventure, Ephraim Sidon and Rony Oren; Scopus Films (Ltd.) London, 1986

The Animated Haggadah, Rony Oren; Scopus Films (Ltd.) London, 1989

The Animated Menorah: Travels on a Space Dreidel, Rony Oren and Ephraim Sidon; Scopus Films (Ltd.) London, 1986

The Animated Israel: a Homecoming, Ephraim Sidon, Hanah Kaminski and Gil Elkabetz; Scopus Films (Ltd.) London, 1987

Ask Another Question: the Story and Meaning of Passover, Miriam Chaikin; Clarion Books, 1985

Who Knows One? A Book of Jewish Numbers, Yaffa Ganz; Feldheim Publishers, 1986

Passover A-Z, Smadar Shir Sidi; Adama Books, 1989

Yiddish Proverbs, edited by Hanan J. Ayalti; Schocken Books, 1976

Fiction

Honi and his Magic Circle, Phillis Gershator; Jewish Publication Society of America, 1979

The House on the Roof: a Sukkot story, David Adler; Kar-Ben Copies, Inc., 1976

Not Yet, Elijah!, Harriet Feder; Kar-Ben Copies, Inc., 1988

Holiday Tales of Sholom Aleichem, Sholom Aleichem, selected and translated by Aliza Shevrin; Macmillan, 1985

When Shlemiel went to Warsaw and other stories, Isaac Bashevis Singer, translated by the author and Elizabeth Shub; Collins, 1988

Does God have a Big Toe? Stories about Stories in the Bible, Marc Gellman, paintings by Oscar de Mejo; HarpersCollins Publishers, 1993

Tanta Teva and the Magic Booth, Joel Lurie Grishaver; Alef Design Group, 1992

The Tattooed Torah, Marvell Ginsburg; Union of American Hebrew Congregations, 1983

The Aleph-Bet Story Book, Deborah Pessin; The Jewish Publication Society of America, 1990

Are You There, God? It's me, Margaret, Judy Blume; Pan, 1990

Emma Ansky-Levine and her Mitzvah Machine, Lawrence Bush; Union of American Hebrew Congregations Press, 1992

A closer look

This picture shows children wearing fancy dress to celebrate Purim. The children are pupils at a Jewish primary school in England. At Purim the whole school celebrates together and it is not like an ordinary school day at all. There is a Megillah reading and a party, and everyone wears fancy dress. Like these children, some Jews who are going to synagogue at Purim like to dress as Ester or Mordehai because they were the heroine and the hero of the story (see pages 28–29). Others prefer to be a character from another story or film – or just anything that seems funny! Sometimes at Purim, men dress as women and women dress as men.

Index